FOR AFTERNOON TEA

Tablecloth
Instructions on page 34.   180cm in diameter.

Square Table Center
Instructions on page 35. 54cm square.

Ruffled Pillow Covers
Instructions on page 36. 41cm square.

Hexagon Table Center

Instructions on page 38.   One side of hexagon, 41cm.

Coasters

Instructions on page 39.   11cm in diameter.

Motif Table Center
Instructions on page 39.   One side of diamond, 40cm.

Square Doily and Matching Coasters
Instructions on page 40.
Doily, 22cm square. Coaster, 10.5cm in diameter.

Flower Motif Tablecloth

Instructions on page 42.   One side of hexagon, 70cm.

Decorate Your Home with Crochet Lace

Rose Tablecloth
Instructions on page 44.   164cm by 118cm.

Radiant Table Center
Instructions on page 46.   106cm in diameter.

Floral Table Center
Instructions on page 43.   120cm by 80cm.

Thistle Table Center Instructions on page 48. 58cm in diameter.

Irish Lace Panel
Instructions on page 51. 28cm in diameter.

Thunderbird Runner Instructions on page 55. 90cm by 33cm.

House Pillow Covers   Instructions on page 60.   41cm square.

Animal Wall Hanging
Instructions on page 64. 55.5cm wide and 82cm long.

Butterfly Tablecloth
Instructions on page 61.   109cm by 151cm.

Doily

Sunflower
Instructions on page 66.
43cm in diameter.

Doily

Irish Rose
Instructions on page 68.
29cm in diameter.

Hydrangea
Instructions on page 67.
29cm in diameter.

Marigold
Instructions on page 70.
23cm in diameter.

Doily

Flower Garden

Instructions on page 70. 29.5cm square.

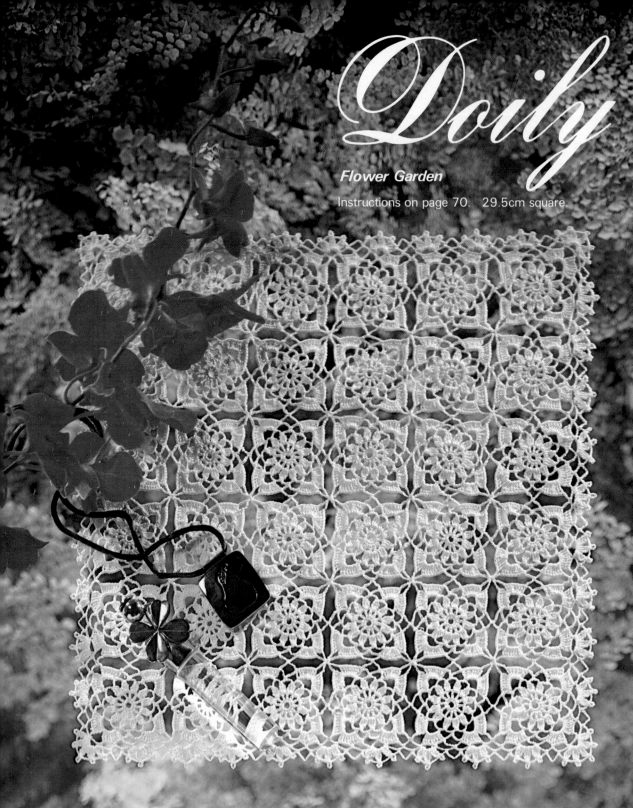

Clematis   Instructions on page 72.   38cm in diameter.

Pond Lily   Instructions on page 73.   35cm in diameter.

Doily

Summer Dream

Instructions on page 74.   39cm in diameter

24

Sand Dollar
Instructions on page 75.   31.5cm in diameter.

Snowflake
Instructions on page 78.   45cm in diameter.

Brighten Up Your Kitchen

Shelf Mat
Instructions on page 76.   Length of lace, 9cm.

Placemats
Instructions on page 77.   25cm by 29cm.

Doily
Instructions on page 78.
21cm in diameter.

Runner
Instructions on page 80.
39cm by 94cm.

Oblong Tray Mat
Instructions on page 80.
20cm by 34cm.

Round Tray Mat
Instructions on page 82.
38cm in diameter.

For Your Bedroom

Mesh Tablecloth
Instructions on page 87.   106cm in diameter.

Diamond-patterned Bedspread
Instructions on page 87.   135cm by 223cm.

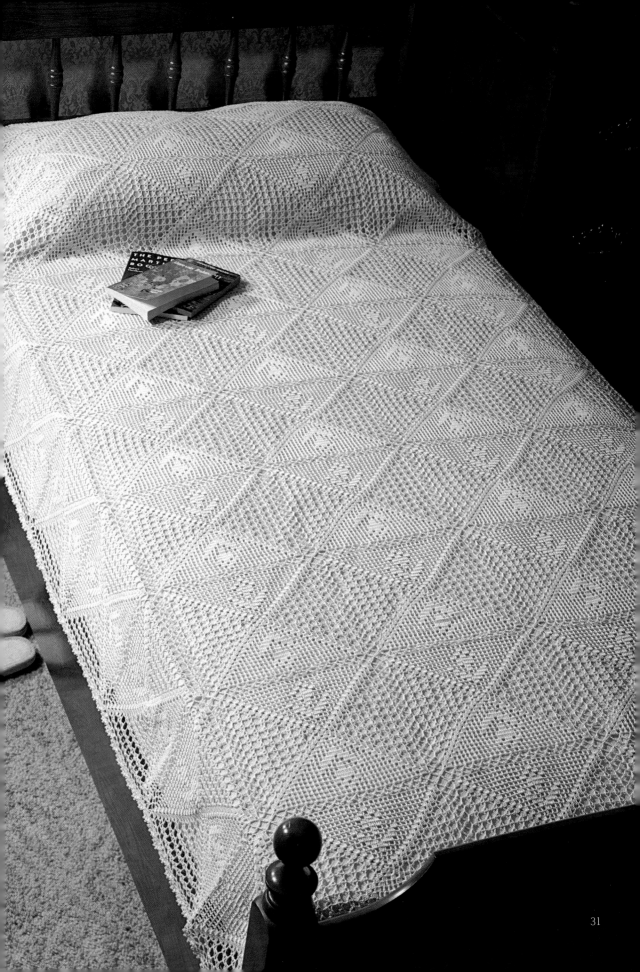

Fret-patterned Bedspread
Instructions on page 86.
152cm by 221cm.

INSTRUCTIONS

Note : All pieces in this book are worked from stitch symbols rather than from row by row directions. The symbols and abbreviations are explained on pages 91-94.

Tablecloth   *shown on page 1.*

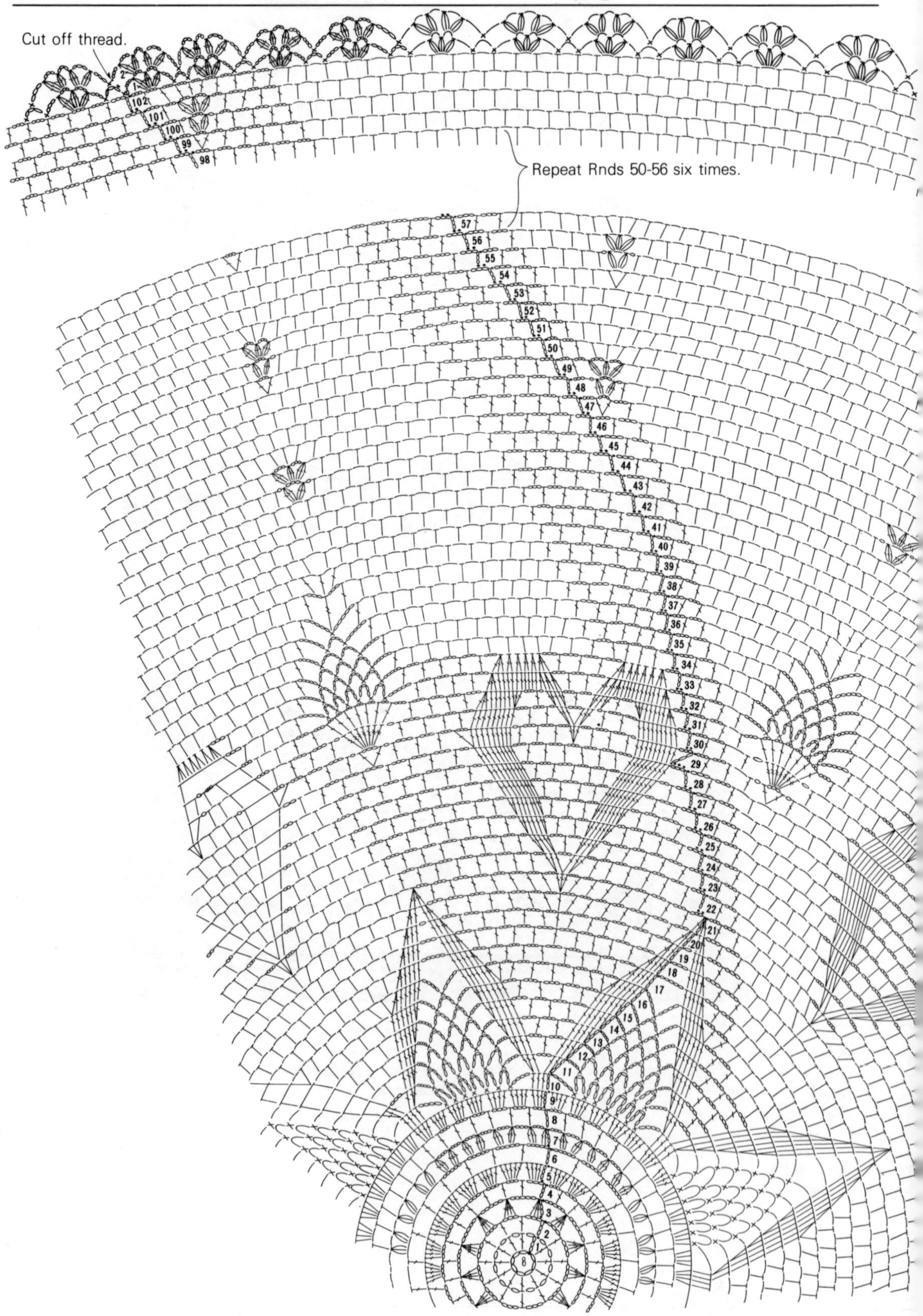

Cut off thread.

Repeat Rnds 50-56 six times.

102
101
100
99
98

57
56
55
54
53
52
51
50
49
48
47
46
45
44
43
42
41
40
39
38
37
36
35
34
33
32
31
30
29
28
27
26
25
24
23
22
21
20
19
18
17
16
15
14
13
12
11
10
9
8
7
6
5
4
3
2

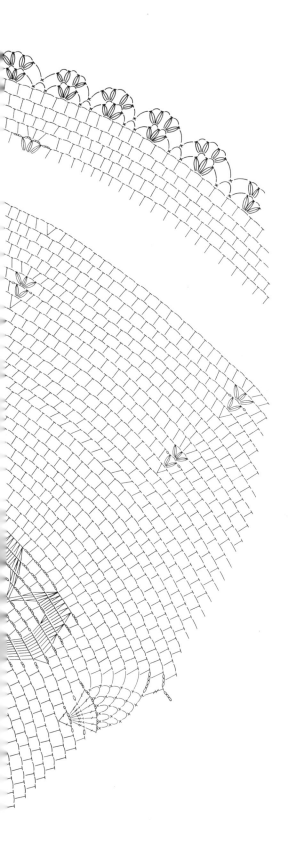

Finished Size: 180 cm in diameter.
Materials and Equipment: Mercerized crochet cotton, No. 18, 500 g white. Steel crochet hook size 1.25 mm.
Gauge: 1 dc = 0.9 cm.
Directions: Ch 8. Join with sl st to form ring. Rnd 1: Ch 3, (ch 1, dc 1) 11 times, ch 1, end with sl st. Rnds 2-56; Work following chart. Rnds 57-102: Repeat Rnds 50-56 six times. Work 2 rnds for edging all around.

Square Table Center

shown on page 2.

Finished Size: 54 cm square.
Materials and Equipment: Mercerized crochet cotton, No. 40, 30 g white. Steel crochet hook size 0.90 mm.
Gauge: 1 dc = 0.5 cm.
Directions: Beginning at the bottom edge ch 250 for foundation. Work in filet crochet for 83 rows following chart. Work 11 rnds for edging all around.

Edging

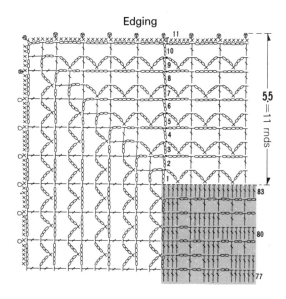

Ruffled Pillow Covers   *shown on page 3.*

Finished Size: 41cm square. Width of ruffle, 4.5cm.
Materials and Equipment (for one): Mercerized crochet
cotton, No. 40, 110g white. Steel crochet hook, sizes
0.90mm and 1.6mm. Blue pillow stuffed with 550g of
kapok.
Gauge: 10cm = 13 bls, 10cm = 13 rows.

Directions: Beginning at center, ch 12. Join with sl st
to form square. Work in filet crochet following chart.
After working 26 rnds, work 16 rnds for back section.
Work 6 rnds for ruffle. Make braid and insert into openwork of 16th rnd of back. Insert blue pillow and tie braid.

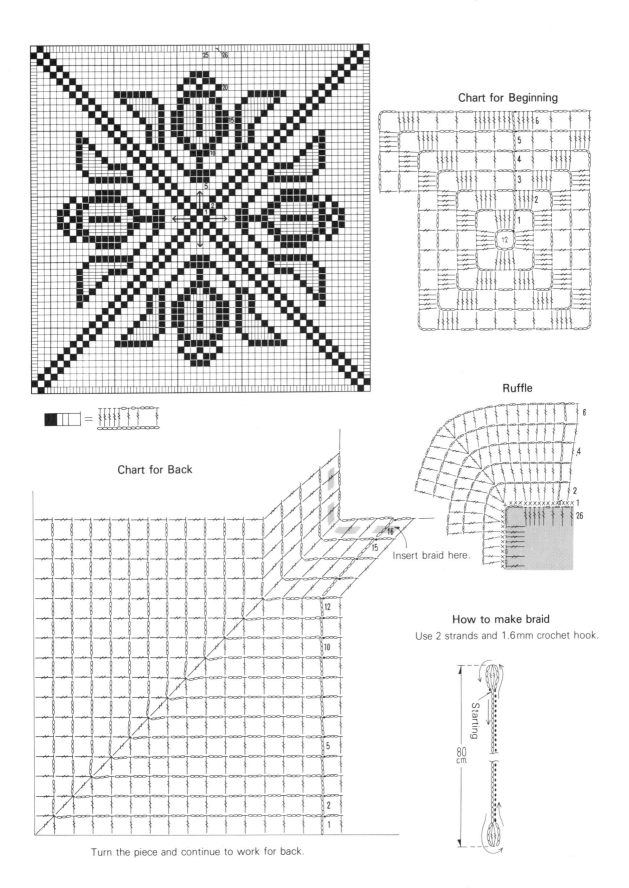

Chart for Beginning

Ruffle

Insert braid here.

Chart for Back

How to make braid

Use 2 strands and 1.6 mm crochet hook.

Starting

80 cm

Turn the piece and continue to work for back.

Hexagon Table Center   *shown on page 4.*

Finished Size: One side of hexagon, 41 cm.
Materials and Equipment: Mercerized crochet cotton, No. 40, 150 g white. Steel crochet hook size 0.90 mm.
Gauge: 10 cm = 17 bls; 10 cm = 17 rows.
Directions: Beginning at center, ch 8. Join with sl st to form ring. Rnd 1: Ch 3, dc 23 in ring, end with sl st. Rnd 2: Ch 3, dc 1, (ch 2, dc 1, ch 2, dc 3) 5 times, ch 2, dc 1, ch 2, dc 1, end with sl st. Rnds 3-68: Work following chart to form hexagon. Work 2 rnds for edging all around.

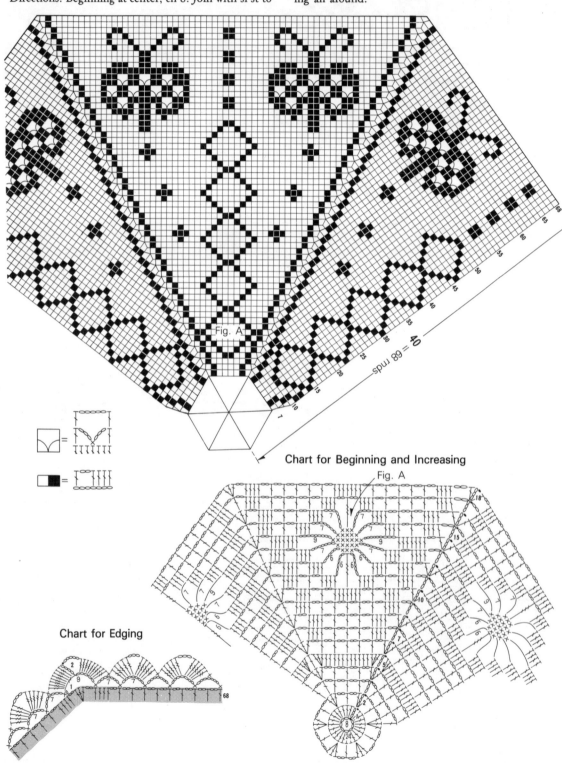

Chart for Beginning and Increasing

Chart for Edging

38

Coasters   *shown on page 5.*

Finished Size: 11 cm in diameter.
Materials and Equipment (for one): Mercerized crochet cotton, No. 40, 4 g white. Steel crochet hook size 0.90 mm.
Gauge: 1 dc = 0.5 cm.

Directions: Make 1p at the end of thread. Rnd 1: Ch 1, (sc 1, ch 4, sc 1, ch 9) 5 times, sc 1, ch 4, sc 1, ch 4, dbl tr 1. Rnd 2: Ch 1, (sc 1, ch 7) 6 times, end with sl st. Rnds 3-10: Work following chart.

Motif Table Center   *shown on page 6.*

Finished Size: One side of diamond, 40 cm.
Materials and Equipment: Mercerized crochet cotton, No. 40, 55 g white. Steel crochet hook size 0.90 mm.
Gauge: 1 dc = 0.6 cm
Size of Motif: One side of hexagon, 4 cm.
Directions: To make motif, ch 7, join with sl st to form ring. Rnd 1: Ch 1, sc 12 in ring, end with sl st. Rnds 2-7: Work following chart. Make and join 36 motifs.

Joining Diagram

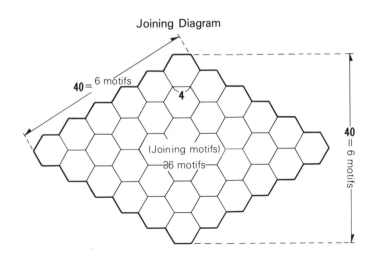

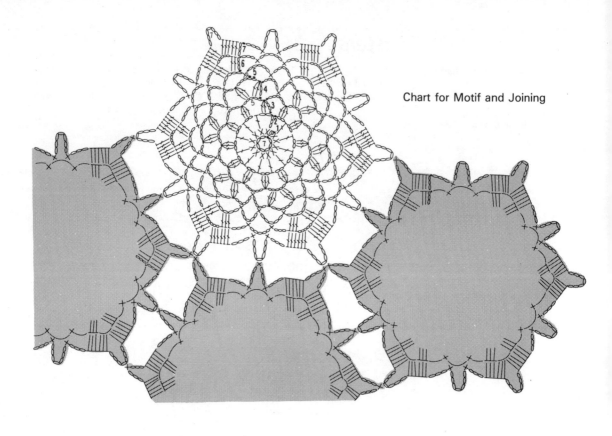

Chart for Motif and Joining

Square Doily and Matching Coasters   *shown on page 7.*

Finished Size: Coaster, 10.5 cm in diameter.
Doily, 22 cm square.
Materials and Equipment: Mercerized crochet
cotton, No. 40, white: 3 g for one coaster: 18 g
for doily. Steel crochet hook size 0.90 cm.
Gauge: 1 dc = 0.6 cm.
Directions: For Coaster: Ch 5. Join with sl st
to form ring. Rnd 1: Ch 1, sc 8 in ring, end
with sl st. Rnds 2-10: Work following chart.
For Doily: Work same as Coaster until Rnd 9.
Work following chart shown on opposite page
from Rnd 10 through Rnd 22.

Coaster

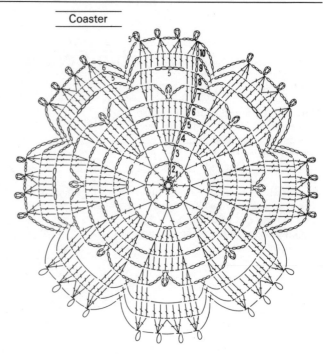

Doily

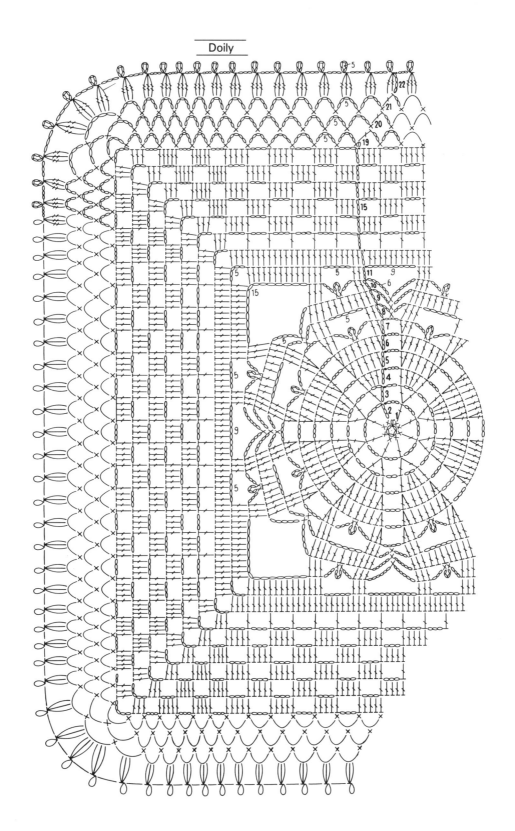

Flower Motif Tablecloth *shown on page 8.*

Finished Size: One side of hexagon, 70 cm.

Materials and Equipment: Mercerized crochet cotton, No. 18, 370 g white. Steel crochet hook size 1.25 mm.

Gauge: 1 dc = 0.9 cm.

Size of Motif: 10 cm by 11.5 cm.

Directions: To make first motif, ch 8, join with sl st to form ring. Rnd 1: Ch 3, dc 23 in ring, end with sl st. Rnds 2-7: Work following chart. Make second motif as for first one, but join with first one on Rnd 7. Make and join 127 motifs in all.

Joining Diagram

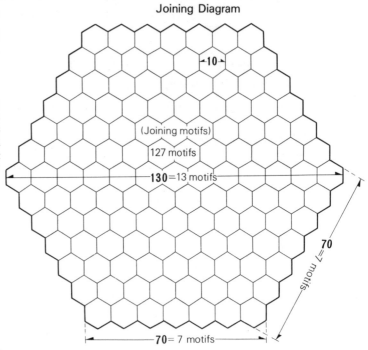

Chart for Motif and Joining

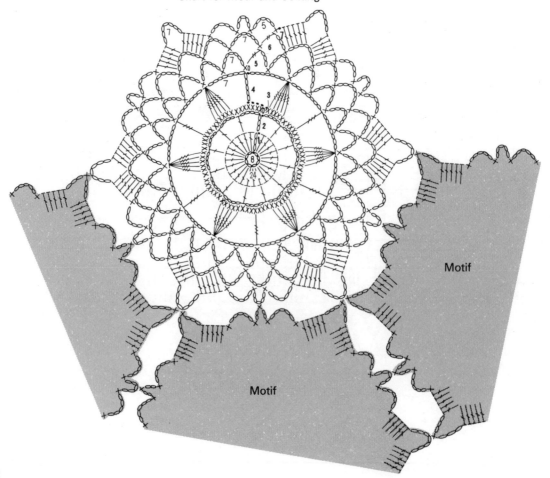

Floral Table Center   *shown on page 11.*

Finished Size: 120 cm by 80 cm.
Materials and Equipment: Mercerized crochet cotton, No. 40, 280 g white. Steel crochet hook size 0.90 mm.
Gauge: 1 tr = 0.7 cm.
Size of Motif: 7 cm square.
Directions: To make first motif, ch 8, join with sl st to form ring. Rnd 1: Ch 4, tr 1, (ch 3, tr 2) 7 times, ch 3, end with sl st. Rnds 2-5: Work following chart. To make second motif, work as for first one and join with first one on Rnd 5. Make and join 173 motifs in all.

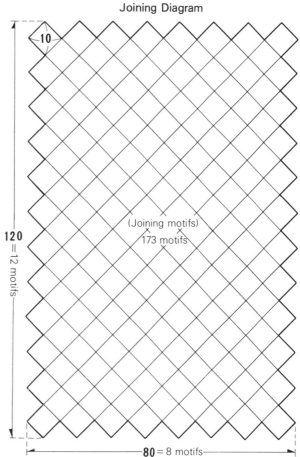

Joining Diagram

10

(Joining motifs)
173 motifs

120 = 12 motifs

80 = 8 motifs

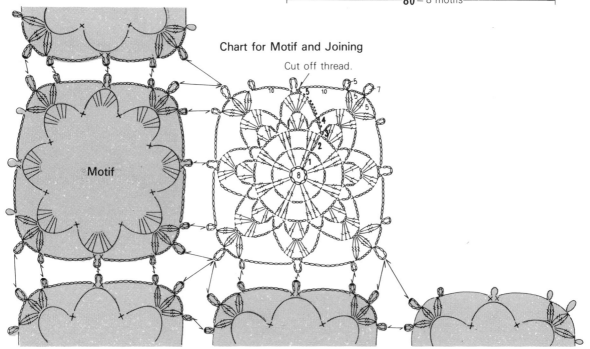

Chart for Motif and Joining

Cut off thread.

Motif

Rose Tablecloth   *shown on page 9.*

Finished Size: 164 cm by 118 cm.
Materials and Equipment: Mercerized crochet cotton, No. 40, 550 g white. Steel crochet hook size 0.90 mm.
Gauge: 10 cm = 20 bls; 10 cm = 20 rows.
Size of Motif: 45 cm square.

Directions: Beginning at the bottom edge, ch 271. Work in filet crochet following chart. Make 6 motifs. Join motifs working 1 rnd of edging around motif. Work 26 rnds for edging all around.

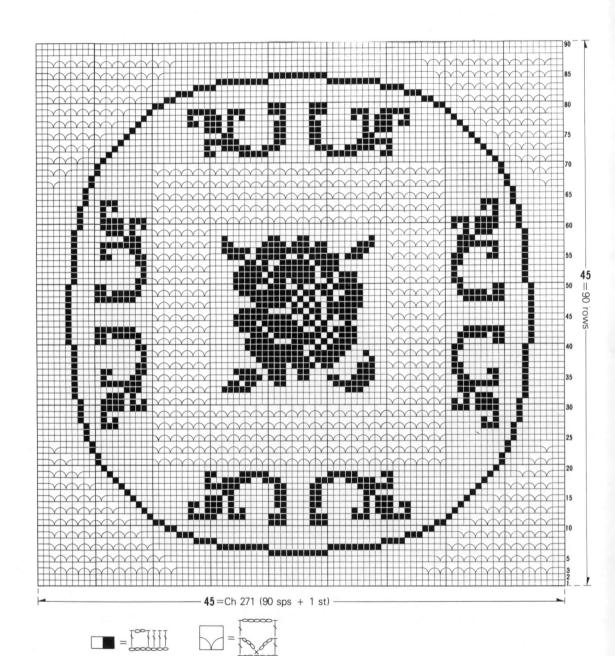

45 = Ch 271 (90 sps + 1 st)

45 = 90 rows

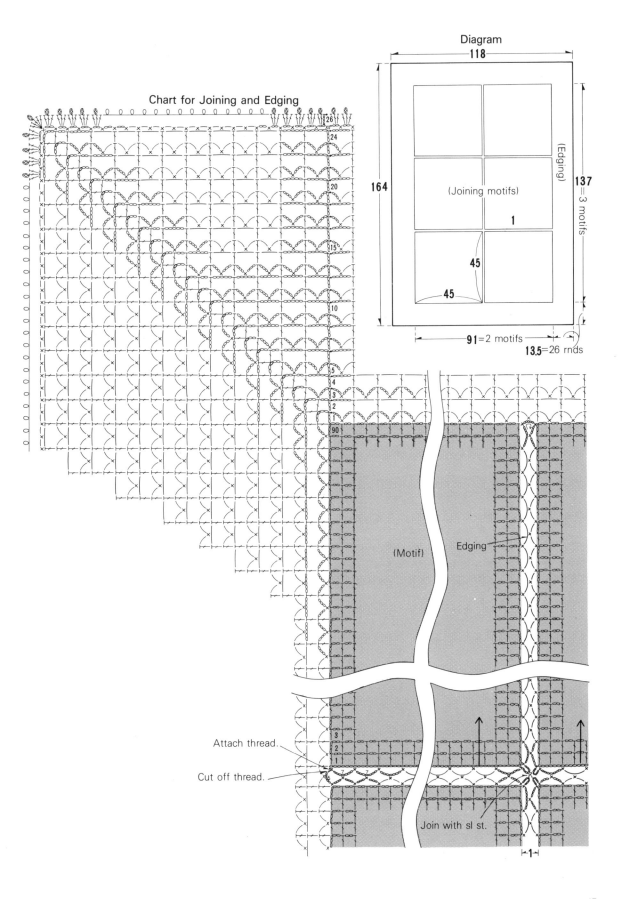

Chart for Joining and Edging

Diagram

118

164

137 = 3 motifs

(Edging)

(Joining motifs)

1

45

45

91 = 2 motifs

13.5 = 26 rnds

(Motif)

Edging

Attach thread.

Cut off thread.

Join with sl st.

1

45

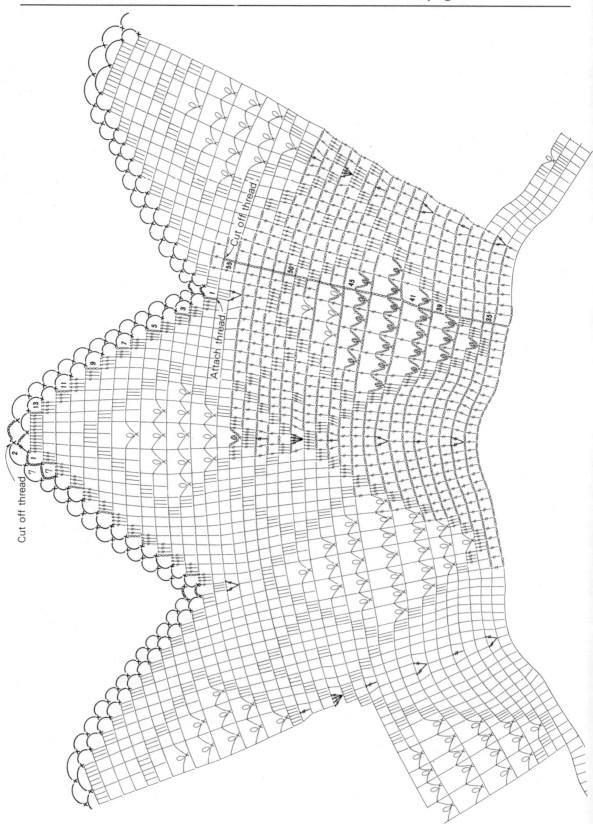

Finished Size: 106 cm in diameter.
Materials and Equipment: Mercerized crochet cotton, No. 40, 190 g white. Steel crochet hook size 0.90 mm.
Gauge: 1 dc = 0.8 cm.
Directions: Ch 6. Join with sl st to form ring. Rnd 1: Ch 1, sc 8 in ring, end with sl st. Rnd 2: Ch 1, (sc 1, ch 18) 7 times, sc 1, ch 9, sextuple tr 1. Rnds 3-55: Work following chart. Cut off thread. To make pointed edge, attach new thread as indicated. Work 13 rows turning each row. Cut off thread. Repeat this for all edges. Work 2 rnds for edging all around.

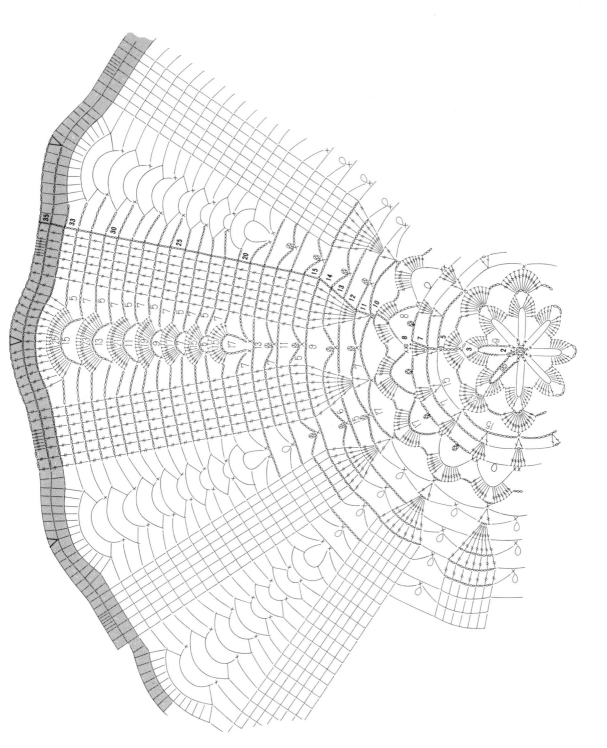

Thistle Table Center *shown on page 12, bottom.*

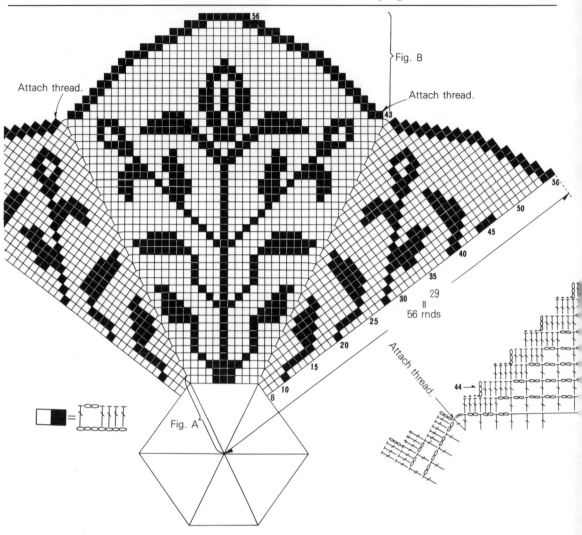

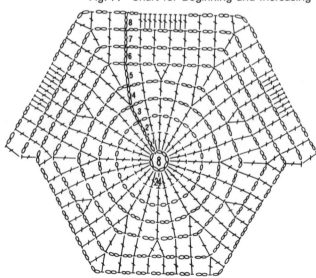

Fig. A   Chart for Beginning and Increasing

Finished Size: 58 cm in diameter.
Materials and Equipment: Mercerized crochet cotton,
No. 40, 80 g beige. Steel crochet hook size 0.90 mm.
Gauge: 10 cm = 19 bls; 10 cm = 19 rows.
Directions: Ch 8. Join with sl st to form ring. Rnd 1:
Ch 3, dc 23 in ring, end with sl st. Rnds 2-42: Work
following chart. Cut off thread. On Row 43, attach new
thread and work following chart. Cut off thread after
finishing Row 56. Repeat Rows 43-56 for remaining sides.

Chart for Decreasing

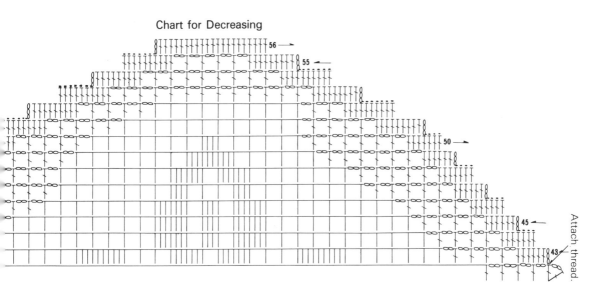

Tulip Table Center   *shown on page 12, top.*

Finished Size: 70 cm by 52 cm.
Materials and Equipment: Mercerized crochet cotton,
No. 40, 150 g white. Steel crochet hook size 0.90 mm.
Gauge: 10 cm = 21 bls; 10 cm = 22 rows.
Directions: Beginning at the bottom edge, ch 304. Work
145 rows in filet crochet following chart. Work 3 rnds
for edging. On Rnd 1 of edging, sc in dc of center of
each side, ch 7 to increase one loop.

Chart for Edging

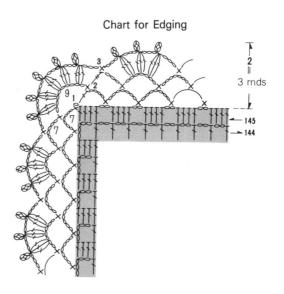

48 = Ch 304 (101 bls + 1st)

Irish Lace Panel *shown on page 13.*

Finished Size: 28cm in diameter.
Materials and Equipment: Mercerized crochet cotton, No. 40, 45g white. Steel crochet hook size 0.90mm. Gauge: 1 dc = 0.5cm.
Directions: Make required number of motifs first—A to K for flowers and (a) to (i) for stems and leaves, following chart. Then make edging. Ch 410 and join with sl st to form ring. Sc 410 each inside and outside of foundation ch. Work 6 rnds in ch and sc for edging. Place edging on cardboard and baste. Place motifs following diagram and baste. Join motifs with ch and picots, but work freely referring to diagram. Remove from cardboard after joining motifs and edging. Then, sew onto background fabric. Place quilt batting under the fabric.

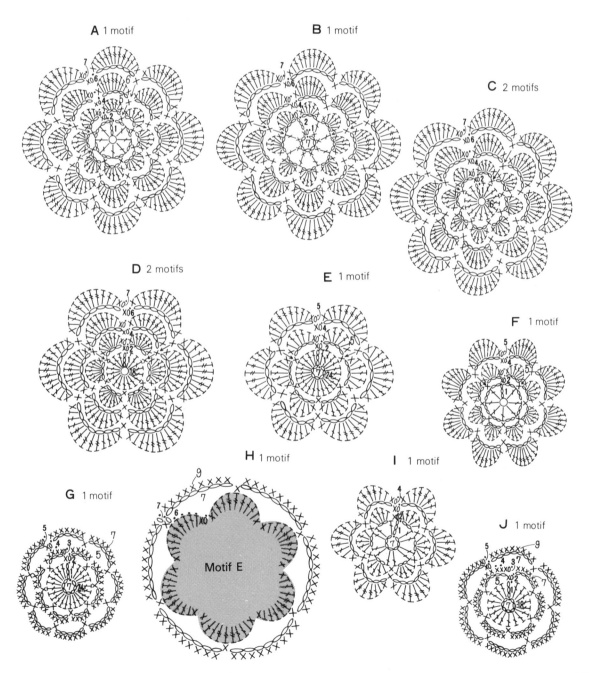

A 1 motif

B 1 motif

C 2 motifs

D 2 motifs

E 1 motif

F 1 motif

G 1 motif

H 1 motif

I 1 motif

J 1 motif

Motif E

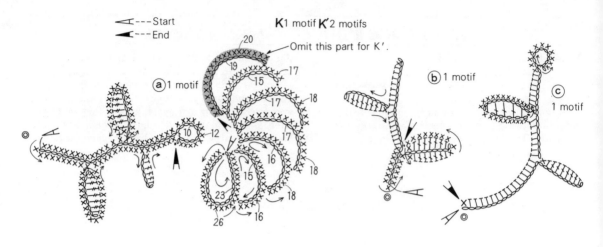

◁---Start
◀---End

K 1 motif **K'** 2 motifs

Omit this part for K'.

ⓐ 1 motif

ⓑ 1 motif

ⓒ 1 motif

Diagram

Ch 410. Join with sl st to form ring.

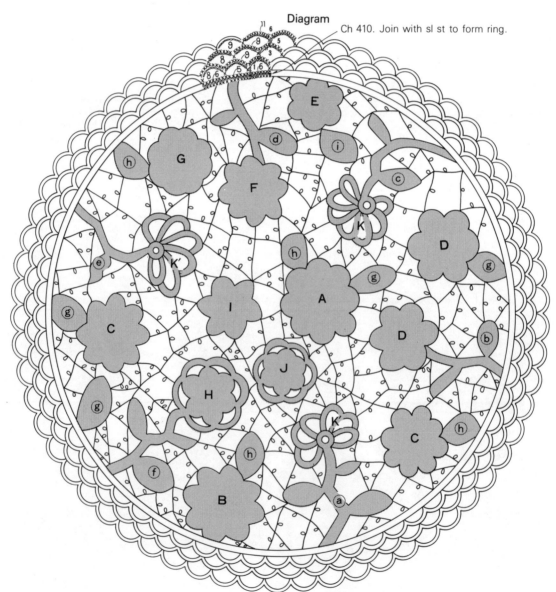

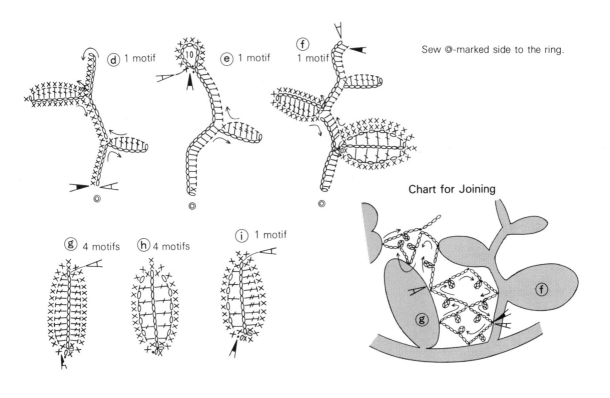

(d) 1 motif (e) 1 motif (f) 1 motif

Sew ◎-marked side to the ring.

(g) 4 motifs (h) 4 motifs (i) 1 motif

Chart for Joining

Piano Cover   *shown on page 14, top.*

Finished Size: See diagram.
Materials and Equipment: Mercerized crochet cotton, No. 40, 280g white. Steel crochet hook size 0.90mm. White linen, 46cm by 162cm.

Gauge: 10cm = 17.5 bls; 10cm = 19.5 rows.
Directions: Beginning at the bottom edge, ch 1249. Work in filet crochet following chart. Turn edges of linen back twice and slip-stitch. Sew finished lace to linen.

Diagram

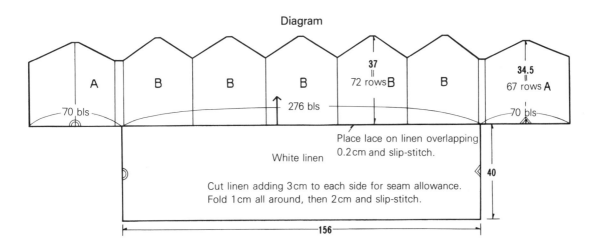

A   B   B   B   **37**
                        ‖
                     72 rows B   B   **34.5**
                                          ‖
                                       67 rows A

70 bls   276 bls   70 bls

Place lace on linen overlapping 0.2cm and slip-stitch.

White linen

Cut linen adding 3cm to each side for seam allowance.
Fold 1cm all around, then 2cm and slip-stitch.

40

156

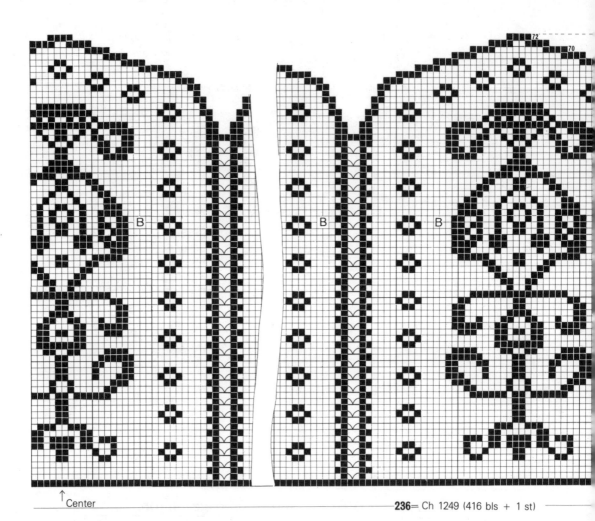

↑
Center

236 = Ch 1249 (416 bls + 1 st)

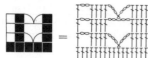 =

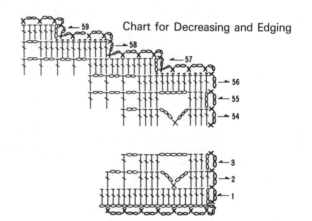

Chart for Decreasing and Edging

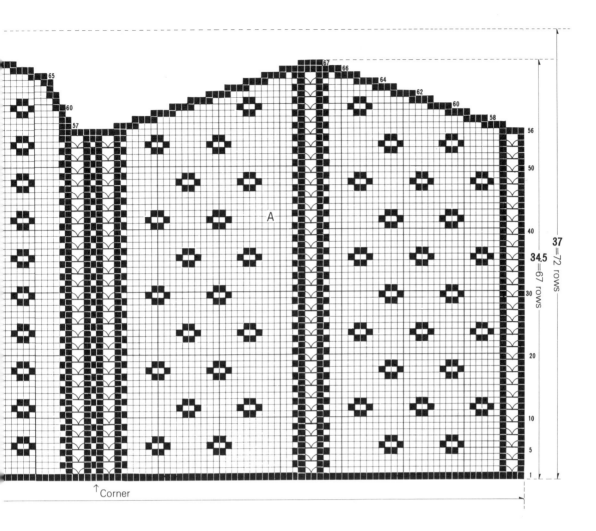

Thunderbird Runner   *shown on page 14, bottom.*

Finished Size: 90 cm by 33 cm.
Materials and Equipment: Mercerized crochet cotton, No. 40, 100 g beige. Steel crochet hook size 0.90 mm.
Gauge: 10 cm = 19 bls; 10 cm = 18 rows.
Directions: Beginning at the bottom edge, ch 190. Work in filet crochet for 166 rows. Work 1 rnd for edging.

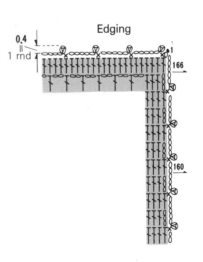

Edging

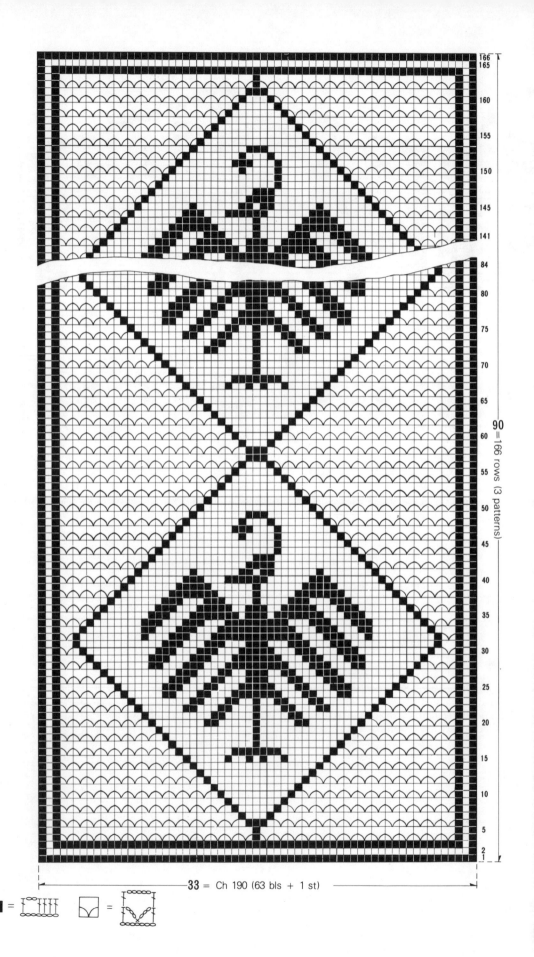

166
165

160

155

150

145

141

84

80

75

70

65

60

55

50

45

40

35

30

25

20

15

10

5

2
1

90 =166 rows (3 patterns)

33 = Ch 190 (63 bls + 1 st)

Building Wall Hanging   *shown on page 15.*

Finished Size: 32 cm wide and 53 cm long.
Materials and Equipment: Mercerized crochet cotton,
No. 40, 65 g white. Steel crochet hook size 0.90 mm.
Dowel, 36 cm long. Cotton cord, 75 cm long.
Gauge: 10 cm = 19.5 bls; 10 cm = 19.5 rows.
Directions: Beginning at the bottom edge, ch 181. Work 105 rows in filet crochet following chart. Work 1 row for edging on both sides and at bottom. Turn 3 rows to back and slip-stitch. Insert dowel in casing.

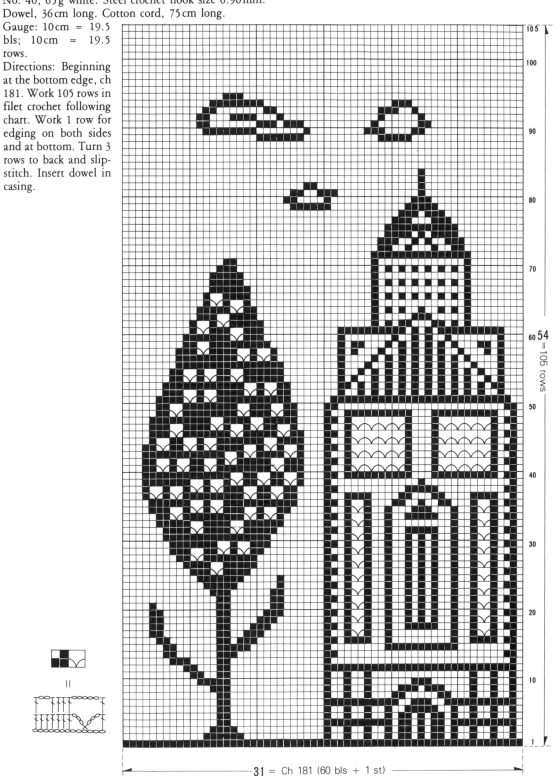

57

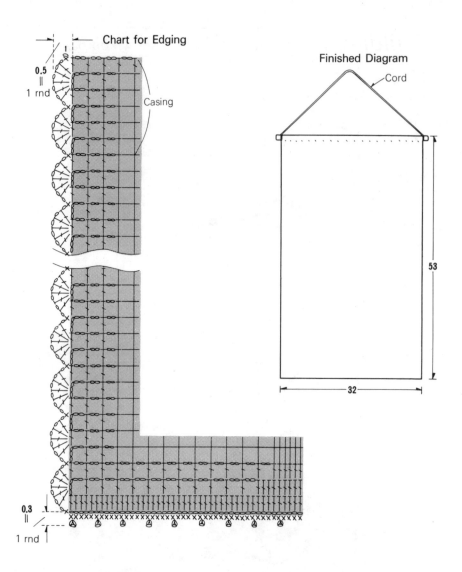

Chart for Edging

Casing

0.5
||
1 rnd

0.3
||
1 rnd

Finished Diagram

Cord

53

32

Table Center *shown on page 16, top.*

Finished Size: 47 cm by 79 cm.
Materials and Equipment: Mercerized crochet cotton,
No. 40, 130 g white. Steel crochet hook size 0.90 mm.
Gauge: 10 cm = 20 bls; 10 cm = 19 rows.
Directions: Beginning at the bottom edge, ch 274. Work
149 rows in filet crochet following chart. Work 1 rnd
for edging.

Chart for Edging

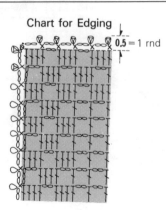

0.5 = 1 rnd

46 = Ch 274 (91 bls and sps + 1 st)

House Pillow Covers *shown on page 16, bottom.*

Finished Size: 41 cm square.
Materials and Equipment (for one): Mercerized crochet cotton, No. 40, 100 g beige. Inner pillow stuffed with 550 g of kapok. Steel crochet hook, sizes 0.90 mm and 1.60 mm.
Gauge: 10 cm = 19 bls; 10 cm = 19 rows.

Directions: Beginning at the bottom edge, ch 235. Work 78 fows in filet crochet following chart. Make 78 sps each for one side and work 10 rnds in filet crochet decreasing as indicated. Work even from Rnds 11 to 17. Make braid and insert into openwork of last rnd. Insert inner pillow.

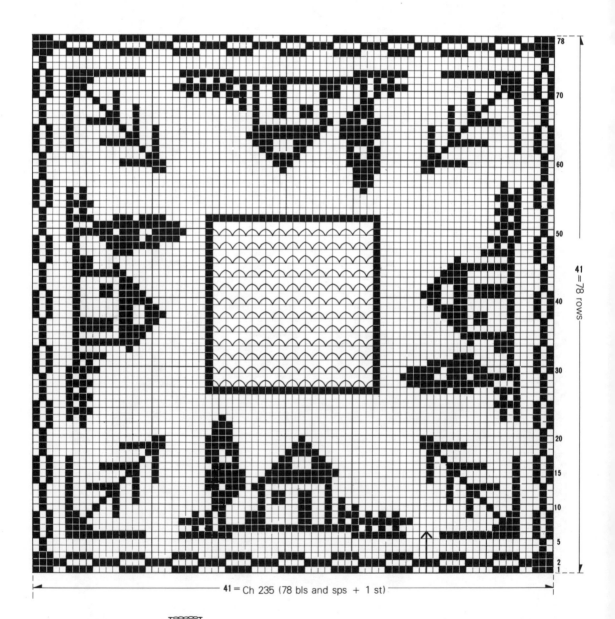

41 = Ch 235 (78 bls and sps + 1 st)

41 = 78 rows

60

Chart for Back

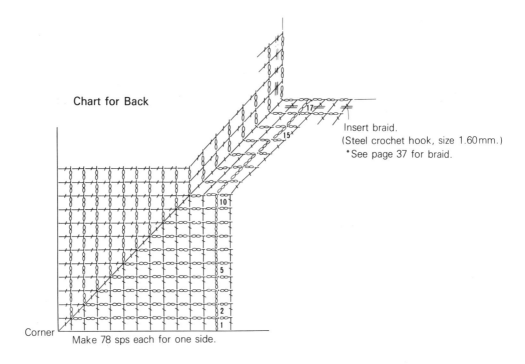

Insert braid.
(Steel crochet hook, size 1.60mm.)
*See page 37 for braid.

Corner

Make 78 sps each for one side.

Butterfly Tablecloth   *shown on page 18.*

Finished Size: 109cm by 151cm.
Materials and Equipment: Mercerized crochet cotton, No. 40, 520g white. Steel crochet hook size 0.90mm.
Gauge: 10cm = 18 sps; 10cm = 19 rows.

Directions: Beginning at the bottom edge, ch 484. Work 257 rows in filet crochet following chart. Work 18 rnds for edging.

Chart for Edging

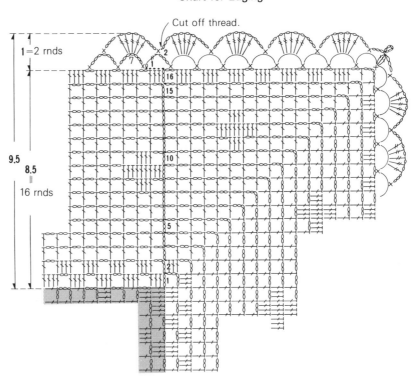

Cut off thread.

1 = 2 rnds

9.5

8.5

16 rnds

132 = 257 rows

80 75 70 65 60 55 50 45 40 35 30 25 20 15 10 5 2 1

90 = Ch 484 (161 bls and sps + 1 st)

Animal Wall Hanging   *shown on page 17.*

Finished Size: 55.5 cm wide and 82 cm long.
Materials and Equipment: Mercerized crochet cotton, No. 30, 160 g beige. Steel crochet hook size 1.25 mm. Dowel, 62 cm long. Cord, 110 cm long.
Gauge: 10 cm = 15 bls; 10 cm = 13.5 rows.

Directions: Beginning at the bottom ege, ch 250. Work 96 rows in filet crochet following chart. Work 1 rnd for edging. Turn 3 rows at top to back and slip-stitch. Insert dowel in casing. Tie fringe at bottom. Tie cord for hanging.

Chart for Edging

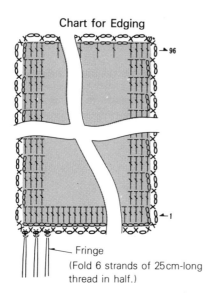

← 96

← 1

Fringe
(Fold 6 strands of 25 cm-long
thread in half.)

Finished Diagram

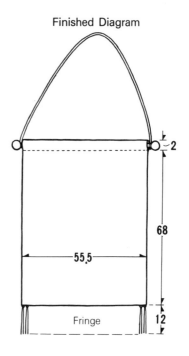

2

68

55.5

Fringe

12

Sunflower   *shown on page 19.*

Finished Size: 43 cm in diameter.
Materials and Equipment: Mercerized crochet cotton,
No. 40, 45 g white. Steel crochet hook size 0.90 mm.
Gauge: 1 dc = 0.5 cm.

Directions: Ch 12. Join with sl st to form ring. Rnd 1:
Ch 3, dc 35 in ring, end with sl st. Rnds 2-23: Work
following chart. Cut off thread. Attach new thread as
indicated and work 9 rows for petal. Make 12 petals in
all. Work 5 rnds for edging.

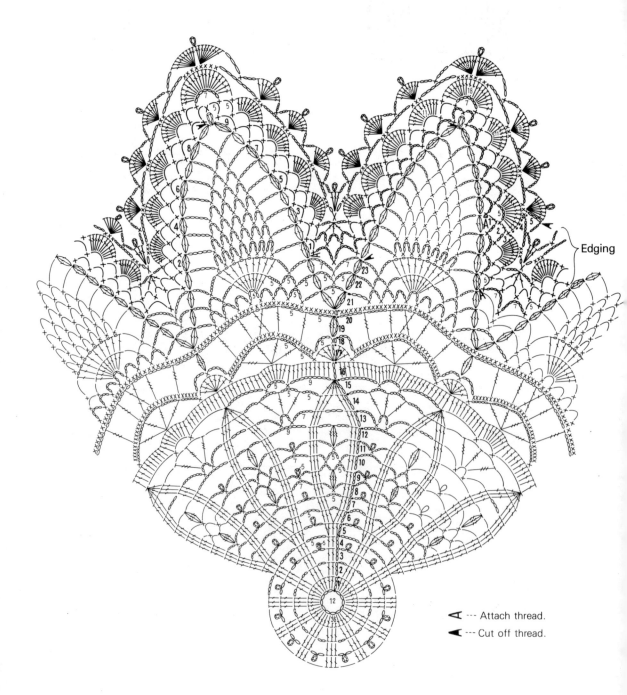

Edging

◁ --- Attach thread.

◀ --- Cut off thread.

Hydrangea   *shown on page 21, bottom.*

Finished Size: 29cm in diameter.
Materials and Equipment: Mercerized crochet cotton,
No. 40, 20g beige. Steel crochet hook size 0.90mm.
Gauge: 1 dc = 0.6cm.

Directions: Ch 8. Join with sl st to form ring. Rnd 1:
Ch 3, dc 23 in ring, end with sl st. Rnds 2-23: Work
following chart. Cut off thread. Rnds 24-26: Attach new
thread and work edging.

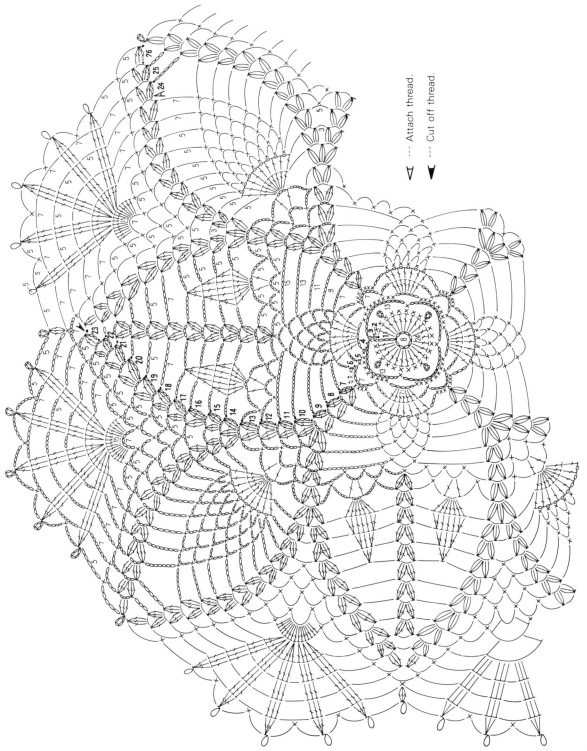

--- Attach thread.

--- Cut off thread.

Irish Rose   *shown on page 20.*

Finished Size: 29 cm in diameter.

Materials and Equipment: Mercerized crochet cotton, No. 40, 45 g beige. Steel crochet hook size 0.90 mm.

Gauge: 1 dc = 0.7 cm.

Directions: To make center motif, ch 8, join with sl st to form ring. Rnd 1: Ch 1, sc 16 in ring, end with sl st. Rnds 2: Ch 1, (sc 1, ch 3) 8 times, end with sl st. Rnd 3: Ch 1, (sc 1, hdc 1, dc 1, hdc 1, sc 1) 8 times, end with sl st. Rnd 4: Ch 1, (sc in back of work between the sc of next 2 petals, ch 5) 8 times, end with sl st. Rnds 5-11: Work following chart. On Rnds 6, 8 and 10, sc in back of work between the sc of next 2 petals. Rnd 12: Ch 1, (sc 1, ch 13) 8 times, end with sl st. Rnd 13:

Ch 1, sc 15 over each loop, end with sl st. Rnds 14-19: Work in mesh pattern (sc 1, ch 5). Rnd 20: Work in mesh pattern (sc 1, ch 6). Rnd 21: Ch 1, sc 7 over loop, end with sl st. Cut off thread. Cut 4 strands of 2 m-long thread. Using these strands as padding, sc over padding twisting as indicated and joining with sl st to Rnd 21. Sl st in sc of underlying padding where two paddings are crossed. Cut off extra padding as shown below. Attach new thread and work 6 rnds in ch and sc following chart. Cut off thread. Make and join 20 motifs. Attach new thread and work 2 rnds in ch and sc. Cut off thread. Cut 4 strands of 350 cm-long thread. Using these as padding, sc over them, twisting as shown.

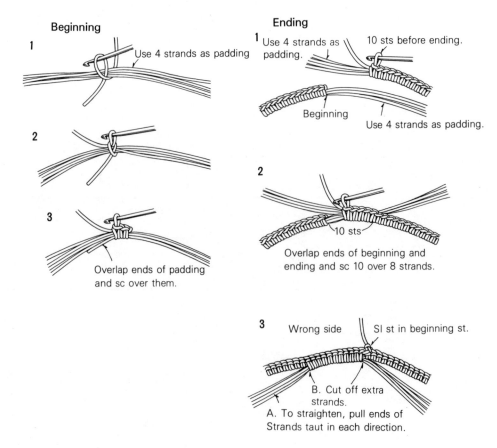

Beginning

1 Use 4 strands as padding

2

3 Overlap ends of padding and sc over them.

Ending

1 Use 4 strands as padding.   10 sts before ending.   Beginning   Use 4 strands as padding.

2 10 sts   Overlap ends of beginning and ending and sc 10 over 8 strands.

3 Wrong side   Sl st in beginning st.   B. Cut off extra strands.   A. To straighten, pull ends of Strands taut in each direction.

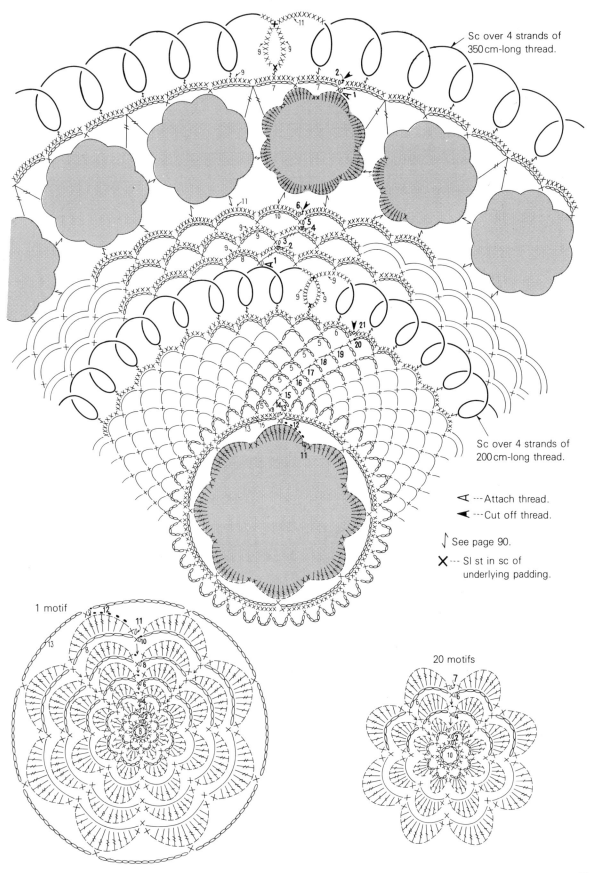

Sc over 4 strands of 350 cm-long thread.

Sc over 4 strands of 200 cm-long thread.

◁ ··· Attach thread.

◀ ··· Cut off thread.

↱ See page 90.

✗ ··· Sl st in sc of underlying padding.

1 motif

20 motifs

Flower Garden   *shown on page 22.*

Finished Size: 29.5 cm square.
Materials and Equipment: Mercerized crochet
cotton, No. 40, 40 g white. Steel crochet hook
size 0.90 mm.
Gauge: 1 tr = 0.7 cm.
Size of Motif: 4.5 cm square.
Directions: Ch 8. Join with sl st to form ring.
Rnd 1: Ch 3, sc 12 in ring, end with sl st. Rnds
2-5: Work following chart. Second Motif: Work
as for First Motif, but join with first one on Rnd
5 in sl st. Make and join 36 motifs. Work 2 rnds
for edging.

Diagram

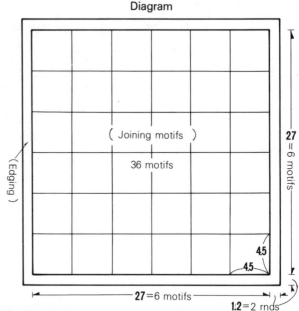

(Joining motifs)

36 motifs

27
= 6 motifs

27=6 motifs

4.5

4.5

1.2 = 2 rnds

(Edging)

Chart for Motif and Joining

Marigold   *shown on page 21, top.*

Finished Size: 23 cm in diameter.
Materials and Equipment: Mercerized crochet cotton,
No. 40, 15 g beige. Steel crochet hook size 0.90 mm.
Gauge: 1 popcorn st = 0.6 cm.

Directions: Ch 7. Join with sl st to form ring. Rnd 1:
Ch 3, dc 4, (ch 4, 5 dc-popcorn) 6 times, ch 4 end with
sl st. Rnds 2-4: Work following chart. Cut off thread.
Cut 4 strands of 110 cm-long thread. Using these as padding

sc over padding, twisting as indicated. Join with Rnd 4 in sl st. Sl st in sc of underlying padding where two paddings are crossed. Then work 11 rnds in mesh pattern. Sc over padding again and join with Rnd 11 in sl st.

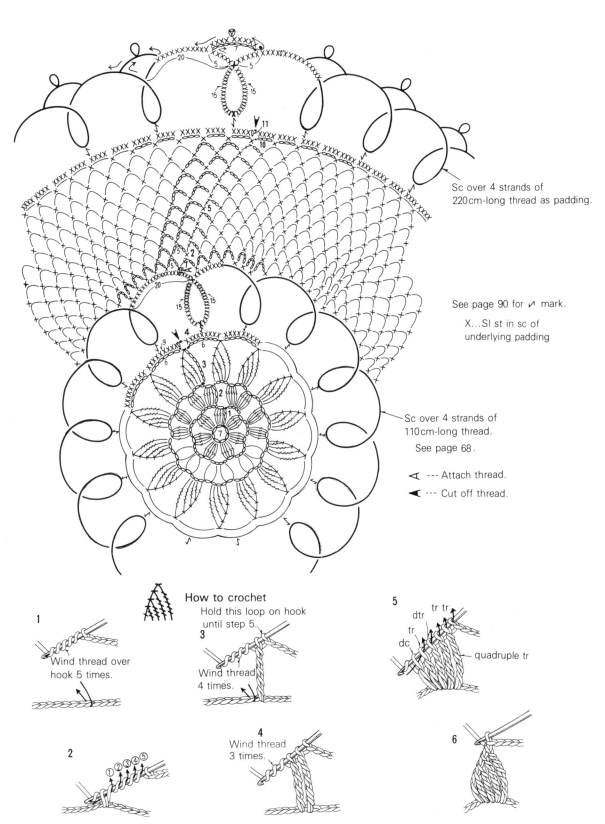

Sc over 4 strands of 220cm-long thread as padding.

See page 90 for ↙ mark.

X...Sl st in sc of underlying padding

Sc over 4 strands of 110cm-long thread.

See page 68.

◁ --- Attach thread.

◀ --- Cut off thread.

How to crochet

1
Wind thread over hook 5 times.

Hold this loop on hook until step 5.

3
Wind thread 4 times.

2

4
Wind thread 3 times.

5
dtr tr tr
tr
dc
quadruple tr

6

Clematis *shown on page 23, top.*

Finished Size: 38 cm in diameter.
Materials and Equipment: Mercerized crochet cotton, No. 40, 35 g white. Steel crochet hook size 0.90 mm.
Gauge: 1 tr = 0.9 cm.

Directions: Ch 10. Join with sl st to form ring. Rnd 1: Ch 4, tr 31 in ring, end with sl st. Rnds 2–4: Work following chart. Cut off thread. Rnds 1–19 (for petals): Attach new thread and work following chart.

Pond Lily   *shown on page 23, bottom.*

Finished Size: 35 cm in diameter.
Materials and Equipment: Mercerized crochet cotton,
No. 40, 30 g white. Steel crochet hook size 0.90 mm.
Gauge: 1 dc = 0.5 cm.

Directions: Ch 8. Join with sl st to form ring. Rnd 1:
Ch 3, (ch 1, dc 1) 15 times, ch 1, end with sl st. Rnds
2-29; Work following chart.

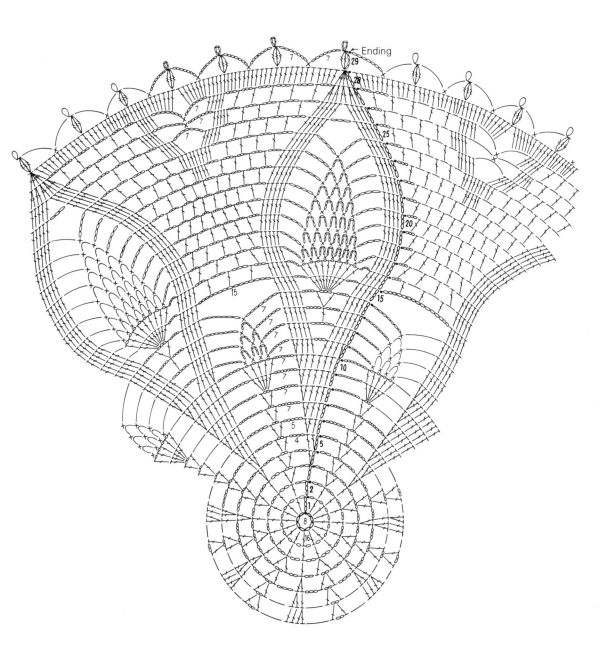

Summer Dream *shown on page 24.*

Finished Size: 39cm in diameter.
Materials and Equipment: Mercerized crochet cotton, No. 40, 30g white. Steel crochet hook size 0.90mm.
Gauge: 1 dc = 0.5cm.

Directions: Ch 7. Join with sl st to form ring. Rnd 1: Ch 1, sc 12 in ring, end with sl st. Rnds 2-37: Work following chart. After finishing Rnd 25, cut off thread. Attach new thread on Rnd 26 and work through Rnd 37.

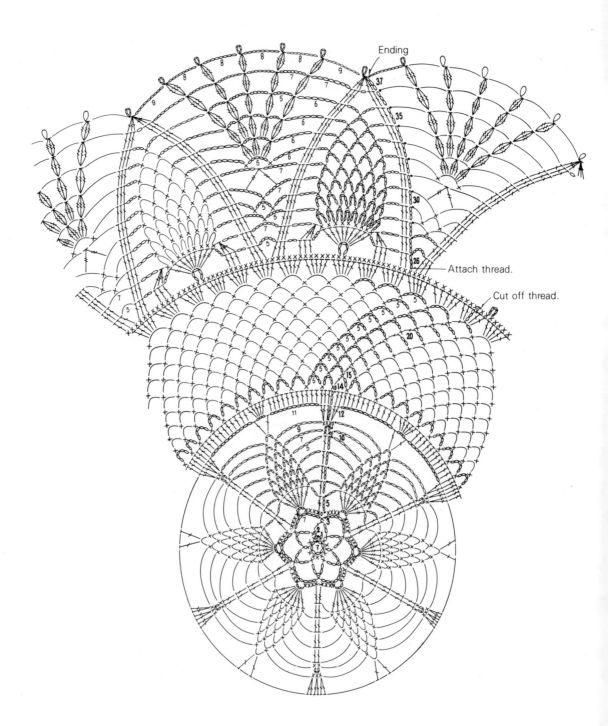

Ending

Attach thread.

Cut off thread.

Sand Dollar *shown on page 25, top.*

Finished Size: 31.5 cm in diameter.
Materials and Equipment: Mercerized crochet cotton, No. 40, 20 g white. Steel crochet hook size 0.90 mm.
Gauge: 1 dc = 0.6 cm.

Directions: (1) To make center motif, ch 12, (dc in each ch) 5 times, (ch 7, dc in dc) 15 times, end with sl st. (2) To make braid, ch 6, (ch 7, dc 2, ch 2, dc 2) all around, but join with sl st as indicated. (3) To make outer motifs, work as for center motif and work another rnd joining with braid in sl st.

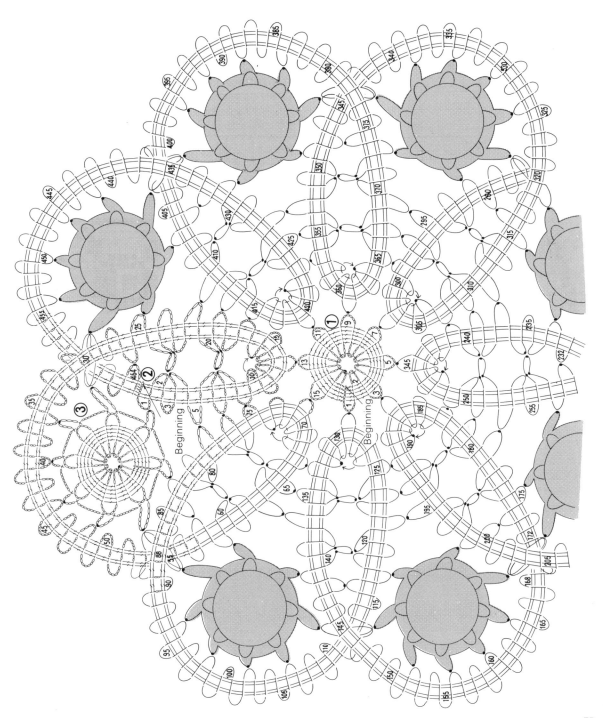

Shelf Mat *shown on page 26.*

Finished Size: Length of lace, 9cm.
Materials and Equipment (for one): Mercerized crochet cotton, No. 40, 30g white. White linen, 23cm by 80cm. Steel crochet hook size 0.90mm.

Gauge: 10cm = 19 bls; 10cm = 19 rows.
Directions: Ch 397 for foundation. Work 16 rows in filet crochet following chart. Work 1 rnd for edging. Sew lace to linen.

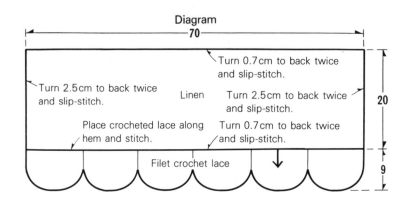

Diagram

70

Turn 0.7cm to back twice and slip-stitch.

Turn 2.5cm to back twice and slip-stitch.

Linen

Turn 2.5cm to back twice and slip-stitch.

20

Place crocheted lace along hem and stitch.

Turn 0.7cm to back twice and slip-stitch.

Filet crochet lace

9

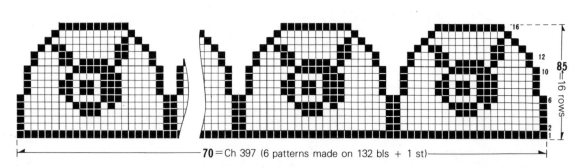

70 = Ch 397 (6 patterns made on 132 bls + 1 st)

8.5 = 16 rows

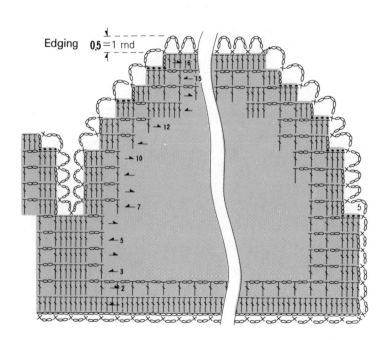

Edging   0.5 = 1 rnd

Placemats *shown on page 27.*

Finished Size: 25 cm by 29 cm.
Materials and Equipment (for one): Mercerized crochet cotton, No. 40, 25 g white. Steel crochet hook size 0.90 mm.
Gauge: 10 cm = 20 bls; 10 cm = 18 rows.
Directions: Ch 142 for foundation. Work 51 rows in filet crochet following chart. Work 1 rnd for edging.

Edging

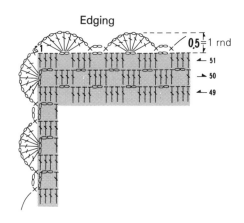

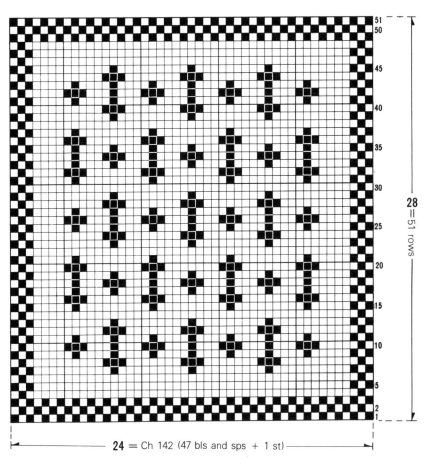

24 = Ch 142 (47 bls and sps + 1 st)

28 = 51 rows

Doily   *shown on page 28, top.*

Finished Size: 21 cm in diameter.
Materials and Equipment: Mercerized crochet cotton, No. 40, 10 g white. Steel crochet hook size 0.90 mm.
Gauge: 1 dc = 0.5 cm.

Directions: Ch 8. Join with sl st to form ring. Rnd 1: Ch 3, dc 23 in ring, end with sl st. Rnds 2-18: Work following chart.

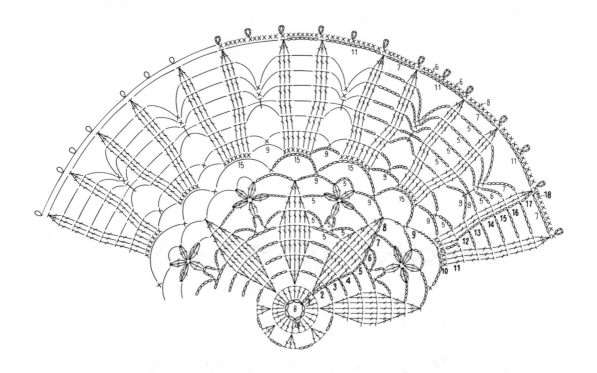

Snowflake   *shown on page 25, bottom.*

Finished Size: 45 cm in diameter.
Materials and Equipment: Mercerized crochet cotton, No. 18, 35 g white. Steel crochet hook size 1.25 mm.
Gauge: 1 dc = 0.7 cm.
Directions: Work in numerical order from 1 to 8 following chart on opposite page.
(1) To make center motif: Row 1: Ch 6, dc in 4th ch from hook, ch 3, dc 2. Row 2: Ch 7, dc 2, ch 3, dc 2. Rows 3-12: Work following chart.
(2) Make second circle. Work 36 rows as for center motif following chart and joining with center motif.
(3) Make outer circle. Work 96 rows following chart and joining with second circle.
(4) & (5) Work as for (1) and (2), but work counter-clockwise. Make 6 pieces and join with center piece as indicated.
(6) Work 156 rows for border, joining with second circles of (5).
(7) Make motifs A joining with second and outer circles.

Diagram

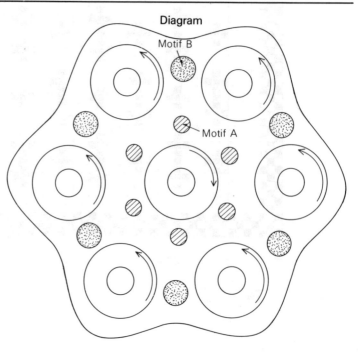

Motif B

Motif A

(8) Make motifs B joining with border,
second circles and center piece.

Runner *shown on page 28, bottom.*

Finished Size: 39cm by 94cm.
Materials and Equipment: Mercerized crochet cotton, No. 18, 140g white. Steel crochet hook size 1.25mm.
Gauge: 1 dc = 0.7cm.
Size of Motif: One side of hexagon, 3.3cm.
Directions: To make first motif: Rnd 1: Make 1p at the end of thread, ch 1, sc 6 in lp, end with sl st. Rnd 2: Ch 3, dc 2, (ch 2, dc 3) 5 times, ch 2, end with sl st. Rnds 3-6: Work following chart. Make second motif as for first one, but join with first one on last rnd. Make and join 102 motifs in all.

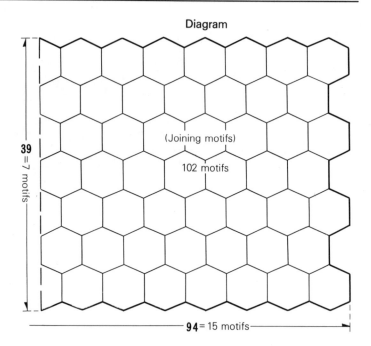

Diagram

(Joining motifs)

102 motifs

39 = 7 motifs

94 = 15 motifs

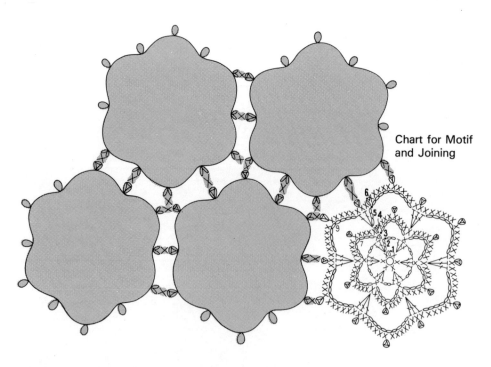

Chart for Motif and Joining

Oblong Tray Mat *shown on page 29, top.*

Finished Size: 20cm by 34cm.
Materials and Equipment: Mercerized crochet cotton, No. 40, 25g white. Steel crochet hook size 0.90mm.
Gauge: 10cm = 20 bls; 10cm = 16.5 rows.

Directions: Ch 79 for foundation. Work 53 rows in filet crochet following chart. Work 3 rnds for edging.

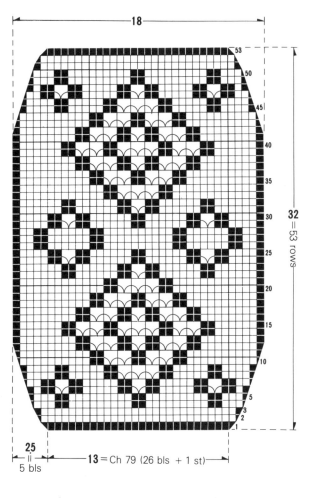

18

32 = 53 rows

25
5 bls

13 = Ch 79 (26 bls + 1 st)

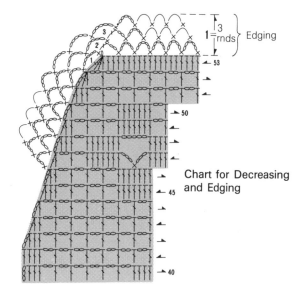

3
2
1

$1\begin{cases}3\\ rnds\end{cases}$ Edging

Chart for Decreasing
and Edging

Chart for Increasing

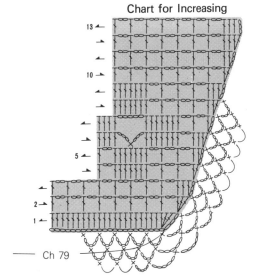

Ch 79

81

Round Tray Mat   *shown on page 29, bottom.*

Finished Size: 38 cm in diameter.
Materials and Equipment: Mercerized crochet cotton, No. 40, 30 g white. Steel crochet hook size 0.90 mm.
Gauge: 1 dc = 0.5 cm.

Directions: Ch 5. Join with sl st to form ring. Rnd 1: Ch 1, sc 8 in ring, end with sl st. Rnd 2: Ch 3, (ch 3, dc 1) 7 times, ch 3, end with sl st. Rnds 3-40: Work following chart and increasing on Rnds 21 and 28.

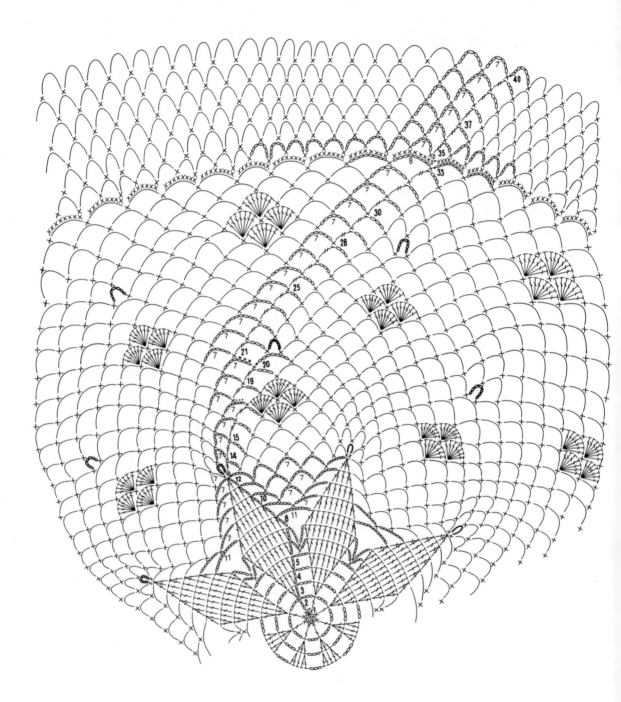

Tablecloth   *shown on page 30.*

Finished Size: 106 cm in diameter.
Materials and Equipment: Mercerized crochet cotton,
No. 18, 160 g white. Steel crochet hook size 1.40 mm.
Gauge: 1 dc = 1.0 cm.

Directions: Ch 8. Join with sl st to form ring. Rnd 1:
Ch 3, dc 2, (ch 3, dc 3) 7 times, ch 3, end with sl st.
Rnds 2-73: work in mesh pattern following chart.

Continued on next page.

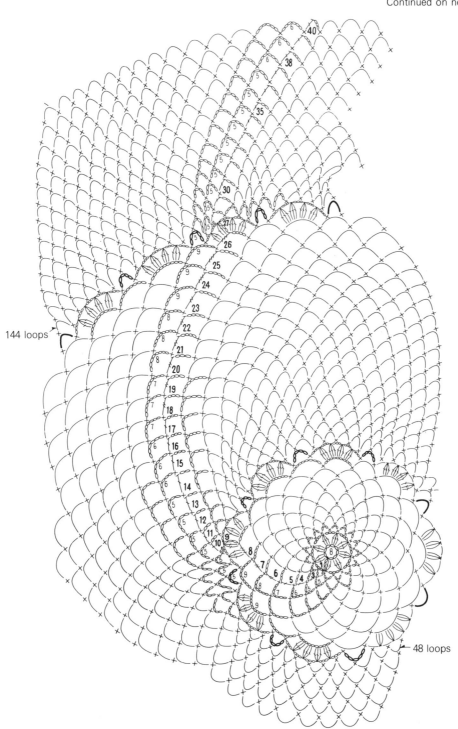

144 loops

48 loops

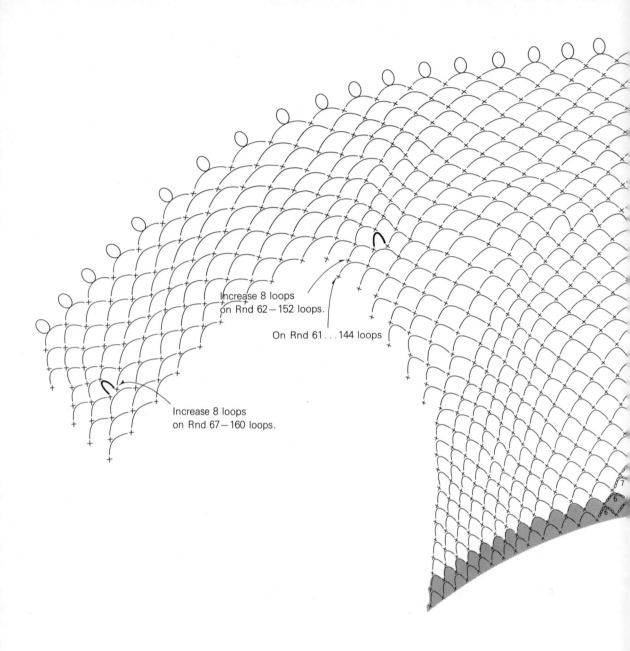

Increase 8 loops
on Rnd 62 — 152 loops.

On Rnd 61...144 loops

Increase 8 loops
on Rnd 67 — 160 loops.

Starting or Turning Chain(s):

On each row or rnd, starting or turning chain(s) is made and counted as one st except sc.
Stitch symbols at right indicate corresponding numbers of starting chain(s). Sc is equal to one ch, hdc to 2 chs, dc to 3 chs and so on.
When working round, end with sl st in top of starting ch of the rnd and make starting ch again on next rnd.

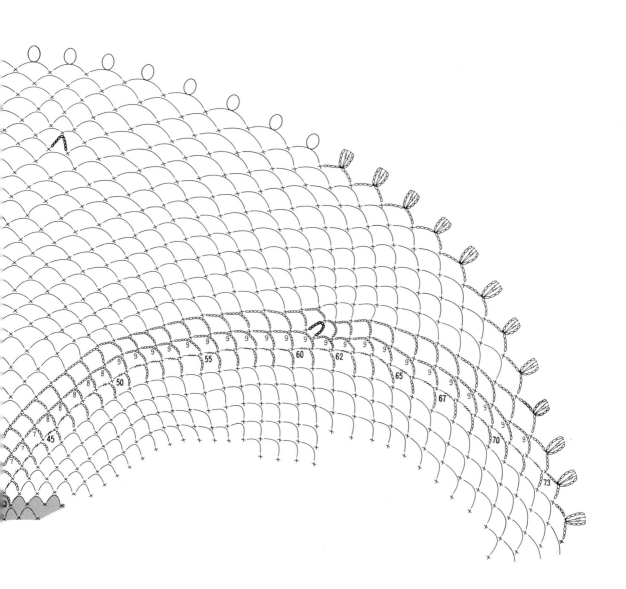

Fret-patterned Bedspread   *shown on page 32.*

Finished Size: 152 cm by 221 cm.

Materials and Equipment: Mercerized crochet cotton, No. 18, 1400 g white. Steel crochet hook size 1.25 mm.

Gauge: 10 cm = 16 bls; 10 cm = 16 rows.

Directions: Ch 139 for foundation. Work 334 rows in filet crochet following chart. Decrease from Row 335 to 344 as indicated. Work 1 rnd for edging. Make second piece as for first one, but join with first one while working for edging. Make and join 5 pieces in all.

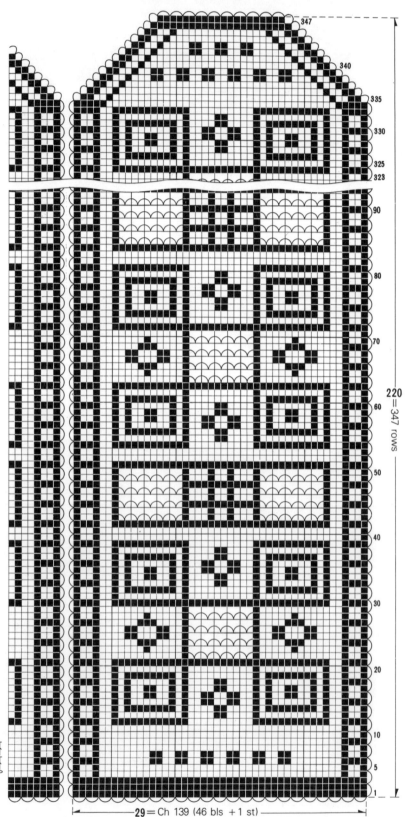

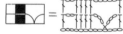

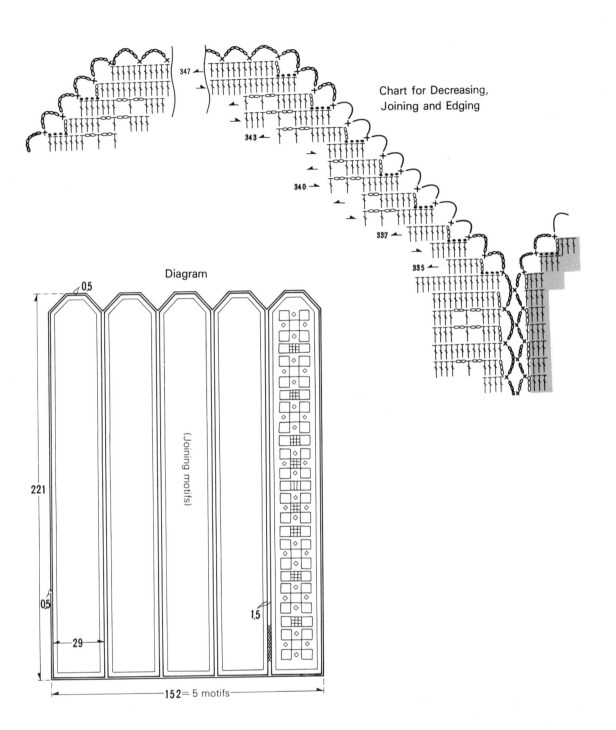

Chart for Decreasing,
Joining and Edging

347

343

340

337

335

Diagram

0.5

(Joining motifs)

221

0.5

1.5

29

152 = 5 motifs

Diamond-patterned Bedspread   *shown on page 30.*

Finished Size: 135 cm by 223 cm.
Materials and Equipment: Mercerized crochet cotton,
No. 18, 1 kg beige. Steel crochet hook size 1.5 mm.
Gauge: 1 dc = 0.8 cm.
Size of Motif: 22 cm square.

Directions: To make first motif, ch 7, join with sl st to
form ring. Work 17 rnds in filet and lacet sts following
chart. Make second motif as for first one, but join with
first one on Rnd 17. Make and join 60 motifs (6 by 10)
in all. Work 3 rnds for edging all around.

Diagram

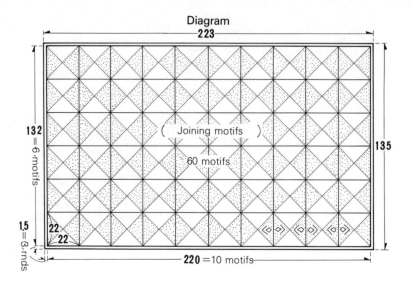

223

132 = 6 motifs   135

Joining motifs
60 motifs

1.5 = 8 rnds   22
22

220 = 10 motifs

Chart for Motif, Joining and Edging

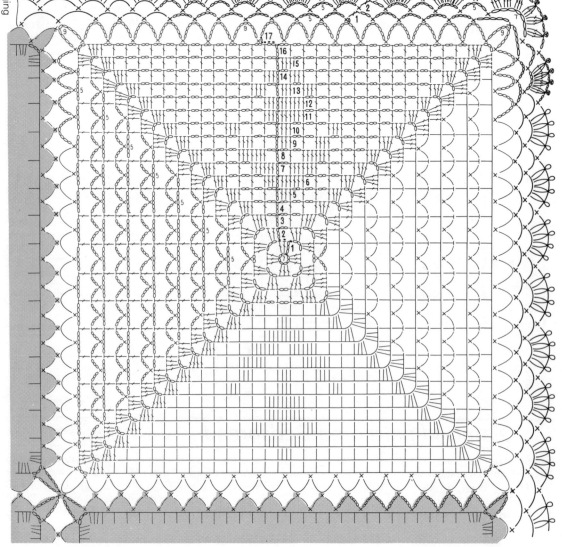

Edging

88

To Begin

 Begin with chain to form ring

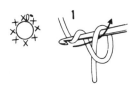 Begin with loop

 1    2   3   4   5

— After working
required sts,
pull end of thread.

Stitch Symbols and How to Crochet

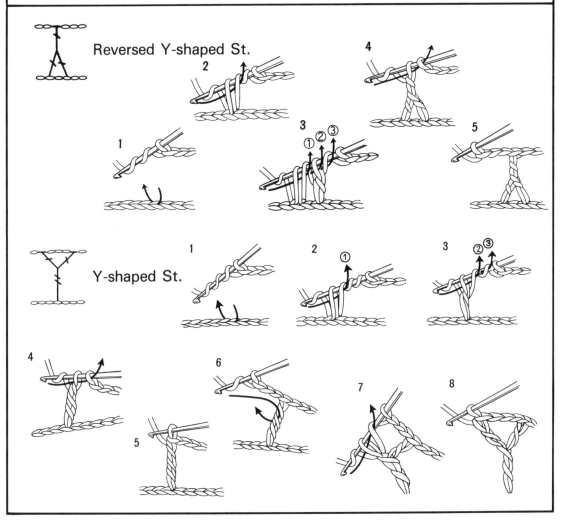

Reversed Y-shaped St.

Y-shaped St.

How to Join Motifs

✿Join while working

(a) Joining by re-inserting hook.

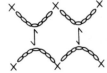

(1) and (2) Ch 3, drop lp from hook. Insert hook in sp of first motif, pick up dropped 1p, and pull thread through 1p.

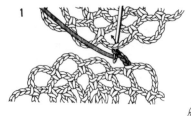

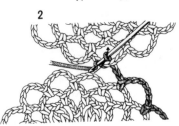

(3) Ch 3, sc over next 1p of second motif.

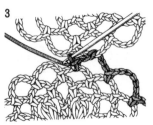

(b) Joining with sl st.

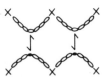

(1) Ch 3, insert hook in sp of first motif, pull thread through ch.

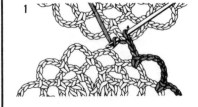

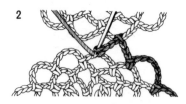

(2) Ch 3, sc over next 1p of second motif.

(c) Joining with sc.

(1) Ch 3, insert hook in sp of first motif and sc.

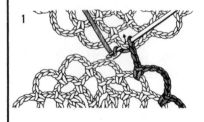

(2) Ch 3, sc over next 1p of second motif.

BASIC CROCHET STITCHES

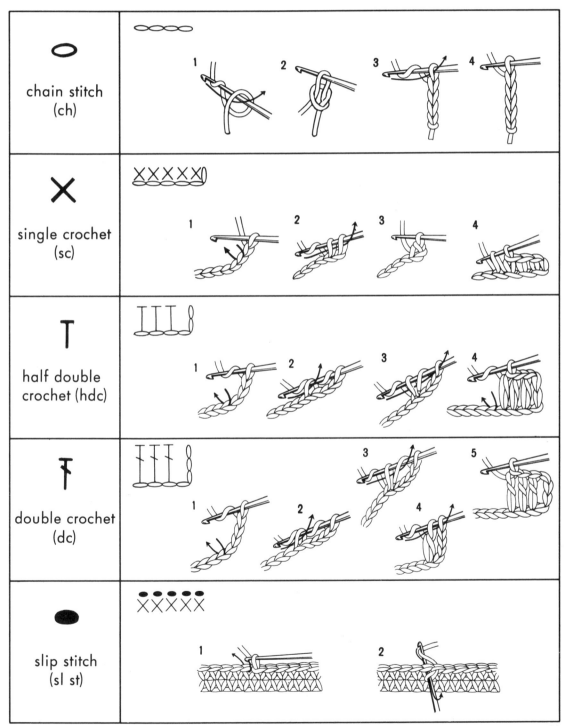

chain stitch (ch)	
single crochet (sc)	
half double crochet (hdc)	
double crochet (dc)	
slip stitch (sl st)	

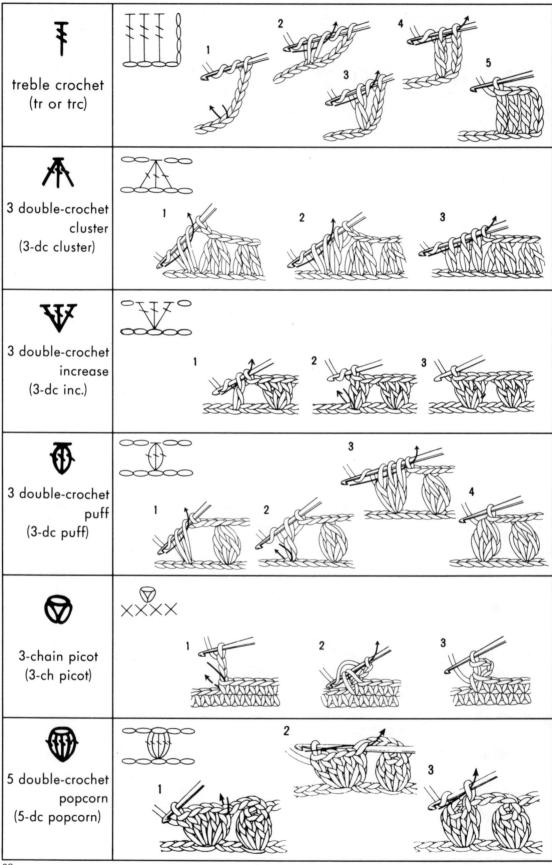

treble crochet (tr or trc)	
3 double-crochet cluster (3-dc cluster)	
3 double-crochet increase (3-dc inc.)	
3 double-crochet puff (3-dc puff)	
3-chain picot (3-ch picot)	
5 double-crochet popcorn (5-dc popcorn)	

2 single-crochet cluster (2-sc cluster)	
3 single-crochet cluster (3-sc cluster)	
1 single-crochet increase (1-sc inc.)	
2 single-crochet increase (2-sc inc.)	
raised double crochet on front side	
raised double crochet on back side	

ABBREVIATIONS

bls	blocks
beg	begin
ch	chain
dec	decrease
dc	double crochet
dtr	double treble crochet
hdc	half double crochet
inc	increase
No.	Number
patt	pattern
rep	repeat
rs	right side
rnd	round
sl st	slip stitch
sps	spaces
sc	single crochet
st	stitch
sts	stitches
lp	loop
tr tr	triple treble crochet
yo	yarn over hook
tr	treble crochet
sk	skip

CM/INCH CONVERSIONS

1 inch = 2.54 cm = $\frac{1}{12}$ foot

1 foot = approximately 30 cm

= 12 inchs

inch	cm	inch	cm	inch	cm	inch	cm	inch	cm
1/8	0.3	5/8	1.5	$1\frac{1}{4}$	3.2	$2\frac{1}{2}$	6.5	8	20.5
1/4	0.6	3/4	2	$1\frac{1}{2}$	3.8	3	7.5	10	25.5
3/8	1	7/8	2.2	$1\frac{3}{4}$	4.5	4	10	15	38
1/2	1.3	1	2.5	2	5	5	12.5	20	51

OUNCE/GRAM CONVERSIONS

As an aid in interchanging yarns, we have prepared the following conversion chart. It lists common yarn amounts and their ounce/ gram equivalents. Please note that these conversions are approximate.

1 ounce = approximately 28 grams
40 grams = $1\frac{1}{3}$ ounces
50 grams = $1\frac{3}{4}$ ounces
100 grams = $3\frac{1}{2}$ ounces

BASIC CROCHET RULES

1. The chain on the hook is never counted as part of a foundation row. For example, if directions say chain 18, You should have 18 in addition to one on the hook.
2. Always insert hook into a chain or stitch from front to back.*
3. Always insert hook under the two top loops of a chain or stitch.*
4. There should be just one loop left on the hook at completion of a stitch or sequence.
*Unless directions say otherwise.

HOW TO FOLLOW DIRECTIONS

The asterisk (*) is used in directions to mark the beginning and end of any part that is to be repeated.
For example "* ch 9, dc 3, repeat from* 4 times" means to work directions after first * until second * is reached, then go back to first * 4 times more, 5 times in all.
When parentheses ( ) are used to show repetition, work directions in parentheses as many times as specified.
For example, "(ch 9, dc 3) 4 times" means to do what is in ( ) 4 times altogether.

YARNS

Crocheting can be done with any stringy material from the finest tatting cotton to raffia, leather cord, or fabric strips. Your choice only has to suit the purpose and be worked with an appropriate hook. Most cotton yarns are mercerized; this means they have undergone a process that strengthens and gives them greater luster. Some also are boilfast, a term that signifies colors will not run or fade in hot water.

If applicable, these terms appear on the label, along with other descriptive information, such as the number of plies that have been twisted together, and sometimes a number (usually between 10 and 70) that signifies thickness of the ply. The higher the number, the finer the yarn. If yarn comes in a skein, it is best to wind it in a ball to prevent its tangling in use.

Whatever type of thread you decide to use, be certain to buy at one time sufficient thread of the same dye lot to complete the work you wish to make. It is often impossible to match shades later as dye lots vary.

For perfect results the number of stitches and rows should correspond with those indicated in the directions. Before starting your work, make a small sample of the stitch, working with the suggested hook and desired thread. If your working tension is too tight or too loose, use a coarser or finer crochet hook to obtain the correct gauge.

CROCHET HOOKS (STEEL)

Continental-mm.	0.6	0.75	1	1.25	1.5	1.75	2	2.5	3
U.S.A.	12	10	9	8	7	6	4	2	1

CROCHET HOOKS (ALUMINUM OR PLASTIC)

Continental-mm.	2.5	3	3.5	4	4.5	5	5.5	6	7
U.S.A.	1/B	2/C	4/E	5/F	6/G	8/H	9/I	10/J	10.5/k

We have referred to McCall's "Needlework & Crafts" and Reader's Digest's "Complete Guide to Needlework" for this page's descriptions.